EXTREME HABITATS

OCEANS

Susie Hodge

Consultant: Jean-luc Solandt, Marine Conservation Society

 **Marine Conservation Society**

The Marine Conservation Society is the charity dedicated to caring for our seas, shores and wildlife. MCS campaigns for clean seas and beaches, sustainable fisheries and the protection of marine life and their habitats. Visit www.mcsuk.org for further information.

Copyright © ticktock Entertainment Ltd 2007
First published in Great Britain in 2007 by ticktock Media Ltd.,
Unit 2, Orchard Business Centre, North Farm Road,
Tunbridge Wells, Kent, TN2 3XF

ticktock project editor: Rebecca Clunes
ticktock project designers: Sara Greasley, Hayley Terry

ISBN 978 1 84696 503 6

Printed in China
A CIP catalogue record for this book is available from the British Library.

Picture credits   t=top, b=bottom, r=right, l= left, f=far
ephotocorp/**Alamy** 13b; **Corbis** Lawrence Manning/Corbis 5b, Bettman/Corbis 8l, Pierre Perrin/Corbis Sygma 25ft, 25ct, Matthew Polak/Corbis Sygma 28, Brandon D. Cole/Corbis 17tl, Bruce Robison/Corbis 16b; D. Weaver/**FGBNMS** 8-9; Flip Nicklin/Minden Pictures/**FLPA** 20b; **Getty** Tobias Bernhard/Getty 10b, Cousteau Society/Getty 12b, Norbert Wu/Getty 16-17; **NASA** 13tr; **National Undersea Research Program** OAR/NURP/Woods Hole Oceanographic Inst 8r; **NOAA** 5c, 9bl, 29bl; Shane Anderson/NOAA 27fb; Doc White/**naturepl.com** 16t; **Oxford Scientific** 21fb; **Shutterstock** 2, 3, 4-5, 6-7t, 6-7b, 7b, 9br, 10-11,10t, 11t, 12-13, 17tr, 17b, 18t, 18-19, 19t, 19c, 20t, 21ft, 21ct, 21cb, 22-23 (all), 24t, 24b, 25cb, 25fb, 26t, 26b, 27ft, 27ct, 27cb, 29cr, 29br, 30, 31, 32; Mike Watson Images/**SuperStock** 1; **Ticktock Media Archive** 5t, 6t, 7t, 11b, 18b, 19b; **VideoRay** 29tr. All artwork Ticktock Media Archive except 4 and 13t Cosmographics.
Front cover Oxford Scientific; back cover Shutterstock

CONTENTS

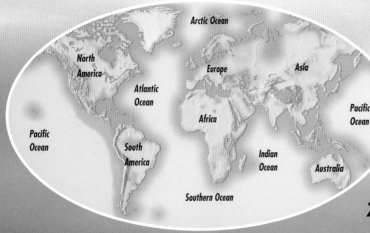

The map shows the world's five oceans.

THE BLUE PLANET

Oceans are massive! They are thousands of kilometres wide and cover 72 per cent of the Earth's surface. This is why our world is often called the Blue Planet.

The world under the water is more extreme than anything on land. Oceans contain the tallest mountains and the deepest valleys in the world.

Oceans affect the Earth's temperature by absorbing warmth from the Sun. Then the constantly moving **currents** spread this heat around the globe, warming land and air during winter.

The crown-of-thorns starfish is found in the Pacific and Indian Oceans. Its spines protect it from predators.

Strange creatures and plants live under the oceans. Some live on the **seabed**, while others spend their lives near the surface. Living in water is completely different from living on land. Ocean animals and plants have special ways of surviving.

OCEAN NOTEBOOK

- The oceans contain 97 per cent of the world's water supply.

- The average depth of the oceans is 3,800 metres.

- The Pacific Ocean covers almost half the surface of the world.

Some fish form big groups called shoals. This is for safety, because shoals confuse predators.

- The oceans contain **minerals** and nutrients washed into them from rivers. Other nutrients come from the creatures that live in the sea.

OCEAN SURVIVAL TIPS

Diving deep underwater causes changes to the brain. Some divers act in odd ways because they are not able to think clearly. Breathing helium and **oxygen** can prevent this.

GOING DIVING

Human beings have evolved to live on land, not in water. Diving is dangerous, even with modern equipment. If you are going underwater, be prepared!

Warm shallow waters are often full of life and very colourful. But sunlight never reaches deeper waters, and so they are cold and dark.

The sea lily is an animal, but it is quite often mistaken for a plant.

All animals need oxygen to live. Fish take in oxygen from the water that moves over their **gills.** We get our oxygen from the air, so divers must take their own air with them. Without air you would quickly lose consciousness, and you would die in minutes.

*A **scuba** diver takes a photo of a **coral reef.***

OCEAN SURVIVAL TIPS

Shark attacks are very rare, but if you are worried by a shark, leave the water as fast as you can. In an emergency, be aggressive. Punch the shark's nose, eyes or gills.

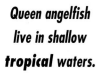

When divers return to the surface after a deep dive, tiny bubbles of **nitrogen** may form in their blood. This is dangerous and very painful. If the bubbles reach the brain, the diver could die. This is called **the bends**. To avoid it, divers surface slowly or go into a **decompression chamber.**

Queen angelfish live in shallow tropical waters.

OCEAN NOTEBOOK

How do you explore the oceans? Well, it depends on how deep you want to go:

• Trained divers can hold their breath and swim down to 30 metres.

• Scuba divers breathe from tanks of air strapped to their backs. They can dive 50 metres down.

• To reach depths of up to 600 metres, divers wear a hard diving suit, like a one-person submarine.

Most submarines can dive about 200 metres below the surface.

• A type of submarine called a submersible is often used for underwater research. Most submersibles cannot dive deeper than about 1,000 metres underwater.

THE DEEPEST PLACE ON EARTH

Map showing the position of Challenger Deep.

The ocean floor is not flat. There are enormous mountains and deep valleys. The deepest known point on Earth is in the Marianas Trench under the Pacific Ocean. The place is called the Challenger Deep and it is 11,033 metres under the ocean's surface.

In 1960, two scientists used a submersible called *Trieste* to reach the bottom of the Challenger Deep. It took *Trieste* five hours to travel down, it spent 20 minutes at the bottom, and travelled back up in just over three hours.

The water pressure at 11,000 metres is enormous. It would feel as if you were being crushed under 50 jumbo jets.

This photo was taken by Alvin at the Hudson Bay canyon, USA. It is about 5,000 metres down.

Until *Trieste*'s journey, scientists believed that nothing could live below 1,000 metres. They thought the pressure, the cold and the dark would make life impossible.

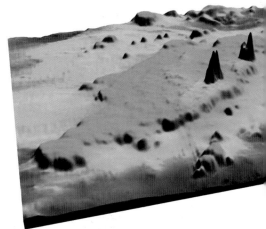

Today, there is no submersible that is able to go as deep as *Trieste*. The deepest-going submersible is *Alvin*, and it only dives to 4,500 metres.

Today's scientists use the submersible Alvin to explore the ocean depths.

Trieste *is being lifted out of the water. It is now in a museum in the USA.*

The scientists onboard *Trieste* were amazed to discover that some animals and plants actually live in the crushing black depths.

Scientists use special equipment to make maps of the sea floor.

OCEAN SURVIVAL TIPS

If you are taking a trip on the *Alvin*, check the weather. If it is too windy, or the waves are too high, it could be dangerous to launch *Alvin*. Your trip will be delayed until calmer conditions.

OCEAN NOTEBOOK

Scientists divide the ocean depths into different zones.

- Sunlight zone – from the ocean surface down to about 200 metres. Most sea creatures live in this zone.

Most ocean life lives in the sunlight zone, as it is only here there is enough light for plants to grow.

- Twilight zone – the area between 200 metres and 1,000 metres. Some light reaches here.

- Midnight zone – from 1,000 metres to 6,000 metres down. It is near freezing and completely dark. This zone usually extends to the ocean floor.

- Deepest ocean – the **trenches** in the ocean floor below 6,000 metres. Very little is known about these remote areas.

THE COLDEST OCEAN

The two coldest seas are the Arctic Ocean and the Southern Ocean. Thick ice floats on top of the Arctic Ocean, covering millions of square kilometres. The Southern Ocean surrounds the continent of Antarctica. So, which is the coldest ocean?

Gentoo penguins live near Antarctica. They can make as many as 450 dives a day, looking for food.

The Southern Ocean is colder than the Arctic Ocean. Currents and winds block warmer air and water from entering it. The Arctic Ocean is open to warmer currents from the Atlantic and Pacific Oceans.

Each winter, the polar oceans freeze over. In the Arctic, this area is about 16 million square kilometres. In the Antarctic, it is about 18 million square kilometres.

When the ice melts in summer, both the Arctic and Southern Oceans are filled with **icebergs**. Only about 10 per cent of an iceberg is above water. This can cause great danger to ships – they hit the iceberg before the crew realise it is there.

A diver swims between two icebergs in the Southern Ocean.

OCEAN NOTEBOOK

- A range of **marine** life can be found in the Arctic and Southern Oceans, including whales, sharks, jellyfish, squid, crabs, icefish and seals.

Beluga whales are white. Their colour camouflages them in the icy Arctic Ocean.

- Polar bears live in the Arctic. They swim from iceberg to iceberg looking for seals to eat. They have partly webbed toes to help them swim.

- Penguins live by the Southern Ocean. Emperor penguins can dive down to depths of 200 metres and stay there for 20 minutes while they hunt for fish.

OCEAN SURVIVAL TIPS

If you are diving in polar oceans wear a very thick **drysuit** to keep you warm. You may also want to wear a harness with a rope to tie you to the surface so you don't get trapped under the ice.

THE LARGEST OCEAN

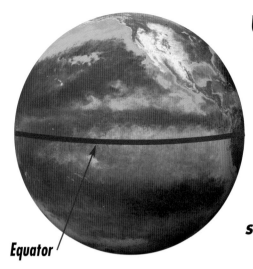

Equator

The Pacific Ocean is bigger than the other four oceans put together and it covers a larger area than all the land on Earth. It's so huge that there's a viewpoint of the Earth from outer space where all you can see is the Pacific Ocean!

The Pacific Ocean. The darker parts of the picture show areas of colder waters.

The Pacific has a greater range of temperatures than any other ocean. Near the **Equator** sea temperatures are about 30°C. Temperatures in the far south of the Pacific, near the Southern Ocean, are near to freezing.

Around the Equator, the Pacific Ocean contains less salt than it does elsewhere. This is because there are many rainstorms near the Equator. The rain brings fresh water to the oceans, making them less salty.

Divers examine an underwater volcano in French Polynesia in the Pacific Ocean. Most islands in this region were originally volcanoes.

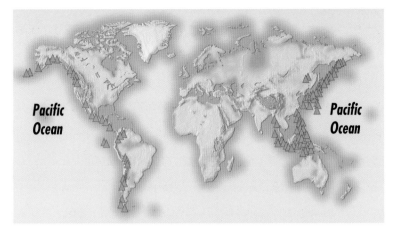

The orange triangles on the map show active volcanoes around the Pacific Ocean.

Pacific Ocean

Pacific Ocean

The Pacific contains more than 80 per cent of the world's active volcanoes. Most occur near the land, forming a circle called the **Ring of Fire.**

Clownfish are one of the most colourful species of fish living in the Pacific Ocean. They can be found along the coast of southeast Asia.

OCEAN SURVIVAL TIPS

The beaked sea snake lives in shallow waters in the Pacific and Indian Oceans. Its bite is deadly. Get medical help immediately if you are bitten by any sea snake.

OCEAN NOTEBOOK

- The oceans and continents are constantly moving. For example, South America is moving west by a few centimetres every year – and so the Pacific Ocean is slowly getting smaller.

A cyclone crosses the Pacific Ocean and heads towards Alaska.

- The oceans are often swept by huge storms, called **hurricanes** in the Atlantic Ocean and **cyclones** in the Pacific Ocean.

- Hurricanes and cyclones travel at speeds of between 160 and 320 kilometres per hour. They can spread up to 950 kilometres across.

THE MOVING SEAS

Waves and currents mean the oceans are always moving. Waves are ripples of water blown across the surface by wind. Currents are large amounts of water which always move in a certain direction.

A massive underwater earthquake in 2004 caused devastating tsunamis in countries bordering the Indian Ocean.

Warm or cold **currents** flow either across the surface of the ocean or deep below it, warming cold areas and cooling warm ones. In the Pacific Ocean, currents are weak, but in the Atlantic Ocean they're stronger. There are seven main currents and thousands of smaller ones.

Many waves are created by the winds. The stronger the wind, the bigger the waves.

Most currents in the top kilometre of the ocean are driven by the wind. Wind creates **friction** with the water, causing currents. The Earth's **rotation** adds to this, creating stronger or weaker currents.

There are sometimes earthquakes, landslides or volcanic eruptions under the sea. These can generate huge waves called **tsunamis**. The giant waves travel at about 800 kilometres per hour and hit the shore with devastating force.

MONSTERS OF THE DEEP

Far under the ocean's surface it is dark and cold, with pressures strong enough to crush a billiard ball. Few creatures live here, so it is hard to find food. The animals that do survive here have become some of the ocean's deadliest hunters.

Viperfish have long fangs. When they bite into their prey, it has little chance of escape.

Like many fish living in darkness, the viperfish can make its own light. It has a row of organs along the side of its body that can produce light. When its prey approaches the light, it attacks!

Although the adult fangtooth looks very scary, it is actually only 16 centimetres long.

The fangtooth fish has been found as far down as 5,000 metres under water. It usually stays in deeper water during the day, where it is safer. At night it swims upwards to find its food of smaller fish and squid.

Hagfish produce sticky slime to protect themselves from predators. The slime covers the predator's gills, so they can't breathe.

Hagfish are found over 1,000 metres below the surface. They attach themselves to passing fish and bury themselves inside the body. Then they eat their victims from the inside out.

Young fangtooth fish like this look very different from the adults. It was once thought they were two different species.

The colossal squid lives about 2,000 metres below the surface. It is one of the world's largest animals, reaching up to 12 metres long. Only one adult colossal squid has ever been caught. Most of what we know about them comes from the remains that have been found inside the bodies of whales.

THE MOST COLOURFUL OCEANS

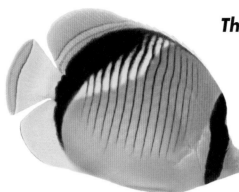

The oceans around coral reefs are full of colour. Coral reefs are formed in warm shallow waters, and are found near many tropical countries. One coral reef may be home to as many as 3,000 species of living things.

This lined butterflyfish will chase away other butterflyfish that swim into its part of the coral reef.

Coral reefs are formed by tiny animals called **polyps**. The polyps use minerals in the sea to make protective outer skeletons. When the polyps die, the skeletons are left, forming coral reefs. The reefs grow slowly – only about as fast as your fingernails!

Sea turtles use their flippers to 'fly' through the water. Many live near coral reefs.

The Great Barrier Reef in the Indian Ocean near Australia is the biggest coral reef. It is 150 kilometres wide and over 2,000 kilometres long.

This red coral is growing on rocks in the Pacific Ocean, near Indonesia.

Brightly coloured fish and thousands of other sea creatures live in the shelter of coral reefs.

There are thousands of species of fish living in coral reefs. Many of them, such as angelfish, clownfish and parrotfish, have bright colours and bold markings.

OCEAN SURVIVAL TIPS

A single sea wasp jellyfish has enough poison to kill 50 people. It's very hard to see in the water. If you swim near the Great Barrier Reef check for warning signs on beaches.

OCEAN NOTEBOOK

- There are many different types of coral. Rose coral looks like roses, and sea fan coral resembles little fans. Brain coral looks just like human brains!

- Coral often grows on the **wrecks** of ships and planes.

- Many fish hide in coral during the day and come out at night to feed. Others hide at night and feed in the daytime!

Seahorses are actually a type of fish. They range in size from 5 cm to 30 cm.

- Seahorses twist their tails around coral as an anchor against ocean currents. If a predator appears, they change colour to match their surroundings.

FACTFILE:

Plant Survivors

Plants need warmth, light and the right balance of minerals to grow. Many plants find oceans an ideal place to live. Plants range in size from the tiny phytoplankton to enormous seaweeds.

Seaweeds often have hollow bumps on their stems. These help them to float in the water.

- Some plants don't have roots or anchors, but drift along in the ocean currents.

- **Phytoplankton** is made up of billions of tiny plants, floating together in the ocean.

- Creatures who eat phytoplankton are then eaten by other animals, so without phytoplankton, there would be almost no animals in the oceans.

- Under some oceans are vast forests of giant seaweed known as kelp.

- Kelp is attached to the ocean floor by root-like anchors called holdfasts. Many fish eat kelp and others hunt for prey in it.

- Kelp is the largest of all ocean plants. Some plants can reach nearly 60 metres high.

- Californian kelp grows fast – about 60 centimetres a day!

Kelp sometimes forms great forests under the sea. They provide a home for many sea creatures.

Animals That Look Like Plants

- **Sea anemones**
  - Look like bright underwater flowers.
  - Can move small distances by sliding slowly.
  - Their 'petals' are actually tentacles that sting any creatures that get too close.

Sea anemones

- **Sea urchins**
  - Small, round creatures covered in spines.
  - Grow up to 10 cm wide.
  - Their mouths are at the bottom of their body, and they scrape algae off rocks for food.

Sea urchin

- **Sponges**
  - Cannot move and they don't have eyes or mouths.
  - Eat through their skin by drawing in water containing tiny bits of food.
  - Sponges live at all ocean depths. The ones in shallow waters are often brightly coloured.

Sea sponge

- Sea grasses look like ordinary grass. They grow on shallow sandy ocean beds often next to coral reefs.

- Manatees are also called sea cows. They graze on sea grass, just like cows do on land!

Manatees are slow-moving, gentle mammals, that spend large parts of their days grazing on sea plants.

FACTFILE:

Ocean Animals

Most marine animals are invertebrates (animals without backbones) such as lobsters, shrimps, worms, jellyfish and tiny microscopic creatures. There are also at least 15,000 species of fish in the oceans.

Spots help fish to blend in with their background and hide from predators.

The shovelnose ray is sometimes mistaken for a shark. Like most sharks, rays are mostly harmless to humans.

- 80 per cent of the world's fish live in the oceans.

- Sharks are a type of fish, and there are over 350 species. Sharks are one of the deadliest hunters in the ocean, with very good senses of smell and sight.

- The pygmy shark is the smallest shark, and it is just 22 centimetres long. It lives in warm oceans at depths of up to 1,800 metres.

- In the darkest zones, many animals create light, by mixing **chemicals** inside their body.

The Pacific cleaner shrimp lives on coral reefs in the Pacific and Indian Oceans.

Other Sea Animals

• Mammals

- Seals, walruses and sea lions are mammals that spend most of their lives in water.
- Whales and dolphins are also mammals although they look like fish. Like all mammals, whales and dolphins breathe air and feed their young on milk.

Dolphin

• Birds

- Penguins have flippers and webbed feet. They swim very fast under the water, twisting and turning to catch fish.
- The wandering albatross is a seabird that spends all of its life at sea, and only comes to land to nest.

Wandering albatross

• Reptiles

- The saltwater crocodile can grow up to eight metres long. It is found in waters around Australia, and it can swim many kilometres from land.
- Some snakes and turtles have also adapted to live in the sea.

Saltwater crocodile

- The light produced by sea animals is mostly a blue-green colour as this can be seen best in water.

- Some creatures give off light constantly. Others flash their lights on and off.

This chart shows some of the reasons why some sea animals produce light.	
USE OF LIGHT	**SEA ANIMAL**
A WARNING TO STAY AWAY	JELLYFISH
CAMOUFLAGE	SQUID
NAVIGATION	LOOSEJAW FISH
COMMUNICATION	OSTRACOD (TINY SHRIMP-LIKE CREATURES)
TRAP PREY	ANGLERFISH

- The anglerfish, for instance, uses a light over its head as a **lure**. When small fish move towards the attractive light, the anglerfish swallows them.

FACTFILE:

Ocean People

For centuries, people have lived on or around the oceans, earning their living through fishing, carrying cargo or passengers, and buying and selling goods.

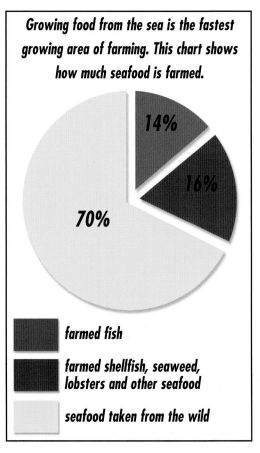

In the past, spices such as pepper, were a valuable cargo for European sailors.

A traditional fishing boat in Tanzania.

- Today, 90 per cent of international goods are carried by ship.

- Half of the world's population lives within 200 kilometres of the coast.

- The first boats were simple **rafts** and canoes. In villages all over the world, small boats still go out to catch fish using traditional methods.

- Sailors in ancient times were often good at finding their way across huge distances, using only the simplest equipment.

- Between the 15th and 18th centuries, European traders sailed to Asia. They brought back gold, silver, precious stones, tea, cotton and silks.

Growing food from the sea is the fastest growing area of farming. This chart shows how much seafood is farmed.

14%

16%

70%

■ farmed fish

■ farmed shellfish, seaweed, lobsters and other seafood

□ seafood taken from the wild

The Moken People

The Moken Year

- The Moken people, or sea gypsies, of Thailand and Malaysia spend seven or eight months of every year in their boats.
- They go ashore during the **monsoon** season and live in simple huts, repairing their boats and still going out to fish when they can.

The boats

- Each boat holds one family.
- The family sometimes dry fish on the rooves of their boats.

Trading

- The Moken people use nets, traps and spears to catch fish, shells, lobsters and other things from the sea that they can use or sell.
- For the few months they are ashore, they trade their ocean goods to buy rice, cooking utensils, oil, nets and fuel.

A Moken man catches a turtle

Moken boats

Pretty shells are collected to sell

- **Pirates** are people who rob ships at sea. 150 pirate attacks are reported every year. Small groups of thieves attack **cargo ships**, taking the money from the ship's safe. They use fast motorboats to get away.

Cargo ships are slow with few crew members. This is why pirates often pick cargo ships to attack.

FACTFILE:

How We Use Oceans

Our oceans have always provided us with food and a means of transport. Today, the seas are more valuable to us than ever before. Oil under the ocean is used for fuel, and the seas are also used for many leisure activities.

Mineral salts from the sea are used in relaxing baths.

- Seaweed is farmed in some oceans and sold as food or fertiliser, or used to make shampoo and ice cream.

- Salt is also farmed from the oceans in shallow waters near the coasts.

Seaweed is even used to thicken some toothpastes.

- Telephone and electric cables are laid underwater. The cables are placed in steel tubes to stop sharks chewing through them!

- Cables are laid on the ocean floor from specially designed ships that carry thousands of kilometres of coiled cables.

OCEAN	Comparing the world's oceans	
	AREA (SQUARE KILOMETRES)	AVERAGE DEPTH (METRES)
PACIFIC OCEAN	103,297,354	4,028
ATLANTIC OCEAN	53,784,276	3,926
INDIAN OCEAN	45,624,902	3,963
SOUTHERN OCEAN	12,630,614	4,000 – 5,000
ARCTIC OCEAN	8,217,310	1,205

Fishing Boats

•Trawlers

- Drag (or trawl) heavy nets through the water or along the seabed.
- Modern trawlers stay out at sea for weeks. They catch many species including cod, haddock, flounder and hake.
- They freeze the fish ready for processing later.

Trawler

• Seiners

- Seiners target open-water fish such as mackerel and herring.
- The net is attached to the boat. It is let down into the water, and **shoals** of fish swim in. The net is then closed and hauled aboard.

Seiner

• Long liners

- Have long lines with baited hooks along them.
- The lines can be up over 1,500 metres in length.
- Long liners can catch fish near the surface such as tuna, or fish that live near the seabed such as cod.

Long liner

- One-fifth of the oil we use is taken from the sea. Ocean **oil rigs** drill under the seabed for oil and pump it to be processed on land.

- Some **archaeologists** spend their lives hunting for and uncovering shipwrecks. The objects they find can tell them more about the past.

Oil rigs can be attached to the ocean floor or float on the surface of the water.

FACTFILE:

Oceans in Danger

In modern times, human activity has greatly increased ocean pollution. The commonest forms of pollution in the seas are industrial waste and human sewage.

Oil spills are a danger to birds, fish and plants. It can take many years for a habitat to recover.

- Chemicals from factories and farms are washed into oceans by rain and rivers.

- If pollution enters the food chain, it can build up and become more dangerous as one creature eats another.

- Litter is another form of pollution. It is left on beaches and washed out to sea.

- Excessive hunting and fishing are putting some species in danger of **extinction**.

- Oil spills are usually caused when large ocean tankers have accidents at sea. The oil floats on the sea's surface, forming an oil slick which can be fatal to many marine species.

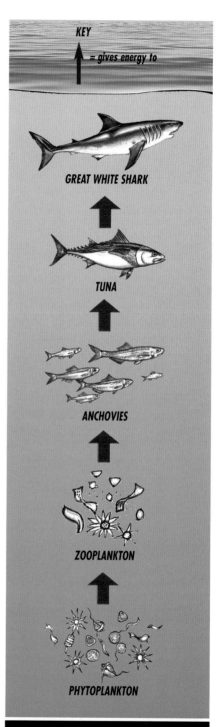

KEY

= gives energy to

GREAT WHITE SHARK

TUNA

ANCHOVIES

ZOOPLANKTON

PHYTOPLANKTON

OCEAN FOOD CHAIN

This simple food chain shows how larger creatures depend on smaller creatures for their food. If pollution affects one link in the chain, it can damage many other animals.

Positive signs

• Protecting the fish

- Many countries have introduced fishing **quotas**, which limit the amount of fish that can be taken from the sea.
- Nets have been changed to allow unwanted fish and dolphins to escape, rather than be slaughtered with the catch.
- Carefully run fish farms may be one answer to people's demand for fish.

• Tourism

- Boat trips to see whales and dolphins, and diving expeditions, are now very popular.

• Creating marine parks

- Some governments have created marine parks. These ares are protected by laws preventing pollution and controlling tourism. The Great Barrier Reef in Australia is a marine park.

Fish farm

Whale watching

Great Barrier Reef, Australia

The white areas on this coral are damaged. This is called coral bleaching, and it is caused by a rise in sea temperatures.

- It is now understood that pollution and **overfishing** are damaging the ocean. Slowly laws are being made to protect this valuable **ecosystem**.

- We have explored only a tiny part of the oceans. There are still many discoveries waiting to be made.

GLOSSARY

algae — simple plants that live in water, many of which are tiny.

anemone — an animal that looks like a plant. It has stinging tentacles to catch prey.

archaeologists — scientists who study the past.

cargo ships — huge, slow ships that transport goods. These ships usually have few crew members.

Challenger Deep — the very deepest point in the ocean. It is 11,033 metres below sea level.

chemicals — substances that can cause a reaction when mixed together. Chemicals made by people are often damaging to the environment.

continent — a huge area of land that contains many countries. Europe, North America and Asia are all continents.

coral reef — structures made from the skeletons of tiny creatures called polyps. Coral reefs are found in warm, shallow waters all over the world.

currents — large portions of water moving in a certain direction.

cyclones — storms in the Pacific Ocean with winds over 160 km per hour.

decompression chamber — a room that slowly returns a diver to normal air pressure to avoid the danger of the bends.

drysuit — special waterproof clothes that keep a diver warm in cold waters.

ecosystem — a particular environment where many varieties of plants and animals depend on each other to survive.

Equator — the imaginary line drawn around the middle of the Earth, dividing it into a southern half and a northern half.

extinction — when a species of plant or animal dies out.

friction — when two things rub together.

gills — the 'lungs' of a fish. Water flows over the gills and the fish takes in oxygen from the water.

Gulf Stream — a warm ocean current flowing up the eastern coast of the USA. Part of the Gulf Stream crosses the Atlantic, bringing warmer seas to Europe.

hurricanes — storms in the Atlantic Ocean with winds over 160 km per hour.

icebergs — masses of ice floating in the sea.

lure — something a predator uses to encourage prey to come closer.

marine — relating to the sea.

minerals — solid substances such as rocks.

monsoon — storms that occur at a particular time of year in some Asian countries.

nitrogen — a gas that is in the atmosphere and our bodies.

oil rigs — structures that drill into the ground to take out the oil that is there.

overfishing — the process of catching so many fish that the fish do not have a chance to make up their numbers.

oxygen — a gas in the air and in water. All animals need to take in oxygen to live.

parasites — animals that live on other animals, taking food from them.

phytoplankton — a mass of tiny plants, so small that each one can only be seen with a microscope.

pirates — people who steal from ships.

pollution — harmful substances in the environment.

polyps — tiny creatures that live in shallow tropical waters. Their skeletons form coral.

quotas — limits on amounts of certain things.

rafts — flat boats made from logs, reeds or plastic.

Ring of Fire — the area around the edge of the Pacific Ocean with many earthquakes and volcanic eruptions.

rotation — the process of something turning around in a circle.

SCUBA — diving with a tank of oxygen. It stands for self-contained underwater breathing apparatus.

seabed — the floor of the ocean.

shoal — a group of fish.

the bends — a medical condition caused by divers surfacing too quickly.

tide — the rise and fall of the ocean which happens about every 12 hours. Tides are caused by the pull of gravity from the Moon and Sun.

trenches — long very deep ditches in the ground or seabed.

tropical — relating to the areas of the world near the Equator where waters are usually between 21°C and 30°C.

tsunamis — huge waves, often caused by earthquakes or volcanic eruptions under the sea.

volcano — a type of mountain which sometimes erupts with hot liquid rock from deep inside the Earth.

wrecks — the remains of ships or airplanes that have sunk to the bottom of the sea.

zooplankton — a mass of very tiny animals.

INDEX